WORDS OF
WISDOM ✥ From
the
CHURCH FATHERS

by
Jimmy Akin

*All booklets are published thanks to the
generous support of the members of the
Catholic Truth Society*

CATHOLIC TRUTH SOCIETY
PUBLISHERS TO THE HOLY SEE

ISBN 978 1 78469 173 8

Contents

Introduction

The Christian faith comes to us from Jesus Christ. During his earthly ministry, by the power of the Holy Spirit, Jesus proclaimed the message entrusted to him by his Father. He then entrusted this message to the twelve apostles, who were witnesses of his earthly ministry, including his death and resurrection.

As such, the ministry of the apostles could not continue indefinitely, but Jesus intended his Church to endure. He said, "You are Peter and on this rock I will build my Church. And the gates of the underworld can never hold out against it." (*Mt* 16:18)

Provision therefore needed to be made for the Christian faith to be passed on to future generations. This was accomplished partly through the writing of the New Testament, but it was also accomplished as the first generation of Church leaders passed from the scene and handed the torch of faith to another.

At the end of his life, the apostle Paul wrote to his young protégé, St Timothy, telling him: "Accept the strength, my dear son, that comes from the grace of Christ Jesus. You have heard everything that I teach in public; hand it on to reliable people so that they in turn will be able to teach others." (2 *Tm* 2:1-2)

The age of the apostles thus gave way to the age of the Church Fathers, which is the hinge connecting the New Testament era to the rest of Christian history.

The Church Fathers are vital witnesses to the Christian Faith. To qualify as a Father, an individual must meet four criteria: he must possess antiquity, orthodoxy, holiness, and the approval of the Church.

An individual possesses antiquity if he lived in the age of the Fathers. In the West, this is usually reckoned as covering the period down to St Isidore of Seville (d. AD 636), and in the East down to St John Damascene (d. AD 749).

Orthodoxy is displayed by individuals who strove to proclaim and defend the Christian message as it had been handed on from Christ and the apostles, without the errors proposed by groups of heretics who came later.

Holiness is reflected in the lives of individuals. Holiness is shown by those who strive to be close to God and to bring others to God. It is shown above all by practising the love of God and the love of one another – the two great commandments that Jesus proclaimed (*Mt* 22:37-40).

The Church has also given its approval to certain individuals by bestowing on them the title "saint." Although everyone who God sanctifies can be called a saint in one sense, the Church recognises that certain individuals have given an outstanding example of holiness in this life and then died in his friendship and gone to be with him in heaven. These are the "canonised" saints whose feasts and memorials are found on the Church's calendar.

Canonisation implies that the Church approves both an individual's holiness and orthodoxy, so for practical purposes, any sainted writer living in the age of the Fathers may be considered a Church Father.

The writings of these individuals are important, and they contain much practical wisdom for living the Christian life.

Other Early Sources

In addition to the Fathers, there are other important Christian writers from this period. Individuals such as Clement of Alexandria, Tertullian, and Origen are not saints, but their writings are still valuable and shed light on how the Christian Faith was understood and practised in their day.

Sometimes we don't have a name to attach to a particular writing. Modern scholars are not sure who wrote first century documents like the *Didache* (DID-ah-KAY) or the so-called *Letter of Barnabas*, but they still provide important windows on the early Church.

This Booklet

In this booklet, we will examine what the writings of the New Testament, the Church Fathers, and other early Christian sources have to say on a variety of subjects.

We will see that the issues we face today have always been part of the Christian life, and that the writings of our Christian forebears have much wisdom from which we can learn.

Jimmy Akin

The Importance of Love

Love is what God cares most about. The first great commandment is to love God, and the second great commandment is to love our neighbour (*Mt* 22:37-40). Jesus said to love and pray even for our enemies (*Mt* 5:44). And John tells us, "He who does not love does not know God; for God is love" (1 *Jn* 4:8).

The best-known discussion of love in the New Testament is found in 1 Corinthians 13, where St Paul indicates that it is not only greater than various spiritual gifts, it is also the greatest of the theological virtues.

While the other two theological virtues – faith and hope – are crucial for our relationship with God, love is the most fundamental. St Paul thus concludes, that "faith, hope, love abide, these three; but the greatest of these is love" (1 *Co* 13:13).

Loving others does not mean that we will always have warm, rosy feelings about them. We will not (cf. *Ep* 4:26). However, love does mean willing the ultimate good of another and doing what we can to help that person be united with God – even if we can only pray for them.

Given all the New Testament has to say about love, it is no surprise that the Church Fathers stress its importance. Thus, early on, Clement of Alexandria picked up St Paul's theme and explained why love is the greatest of the theological virtues:

Faith departs when we are convinced by vision, by seeing God. And hope vanishes when the things hoped for come. But love comes to completion, and grows more when that which is perfect has been bestowed. If one introduces it into his soul, although he be born in sins, and has done many forbidden things, he is able, by increasing love and adopting a pure repentance, to retrieve his mistakes (*Who is the Rich Man That is Saved* 38).

Similarly, St Augustine writes:

The greater the measure in which [love] dwells in a man, the better is the man in whom it dwells. For when there is a question as to whether a man is good, one does not ask what he believes, or what he hopes, but what he loves. For the man who loves aright no doubt believes and hopes aright; whereas the man who has not love believes in vain, even though his beliefs are true. He also hopes in vain, even though the objects of his hope are a real part of true happiness – unless, indeed, he believes and hopes that he may obtain by prayer the blessing of love... This is the true faith of Christ, of which the apostle speaks, "which works by love" (*Ga* 5:6) (*Enchiridion on Faith, Hope, and Love*, 117:31).

Love is thus the ultimate key to the Christian life – and to eternal life.

Daily Prayer

St Paul tells us: "Rejoice always, pray constantly, give thanks in all circumstances; for this is the will of God in Christ Jesus for you" (1 *Th* 5:16-18).

The exhortation to pray constantly does not mean to devote every waking moment to prayer, for that would be impossible, but it does mean that we should pray often.

Prayer draws us out of ourselves. It keeps us from thinking only about ourselves and leads us to think about God (to whom we pray) and others (for whom we pray). It thus helps us fulfil the two great commandments – love of God and love of neighbour (*Mt* 22:37-40).

To encourage us to pray, God has made certain graces contingent on it. Thus neglect of prayer makes life more difficult. As St James says, "You do not have, because you do not ask" (*Jm* 4:2b).

The early Christians understood the importance of regular prayer. After teaching the Lord's Prayer, the first century Christian document known as the *Didache* says, "Pray thus three times in the day" (Ch. 8).

Even when we do not pray using words, the mere fact that we desire something of God becomes a kind of implicit prayer. Thus St Augustine remarks:

> When we have an uninterrupted desire along with the exercise of faith, hope, and charity, we "pray always." But at certain stated hours and seasons we also use words in prayer to God, that by these we may

admonish ourselves, that we may acquaint ourselves with the measure of progress which we have made toward our desire, and that we may more warmly excite ourselves to obtain an increase of its strength (*Letters* 3:130:18).

God knows that we have earthly needs, and he is more than willing to supply them (*Mt* 6:31-33). But even more fundamentally, we have need for union with God himself. Thus St Athanasius comments on how those who engage in regular prayer receive the greatest benefit of all, the Holy Spirit:

Those who are thus continually engaged [in prayer] are waiting entirely on the Lord, and they say, "Let us press on to know the Lord; his going forth is sure as the dawn; he will come to us as the showers, as the spring rains that water the earth" (*Ho* 6:3). For not only does he satisfy them in the morning; neither does he give them only as much to drink as they ask; but he gives them abundantly, according to the multitude of his loving-kindness, giving to them at all times the grace of the Spirit. And what they thirst for he immediately adds… For, "as cold waters are pleasant to those who are thirsty," according to a proverb, so to those who believe in the Lord, the coming of the Spirit is better than all refreshment and delight (*Festal Letters* 20:1).

Perseverance in Prayer

At times in life there are things we want very much – healing for ourselves or a loved one, a new or better job, the lifting of a cross that we have been carrying. Yet when we ask God for these things, they may not be forthcoming.

In the Gospels, Jesus tells the disciples a parable to show that "they ought always to pray and not lose heart" (*Lk* 18:1). In the parable (vv. 2-8), the persistence of a widow causes an unjust judge to finally give her justice.

Some have wondered how Jesus could compare God to an unjust judge, but as St Augustine explains, that is not what he is doing:

> That unjust judge does not in any way allegorically represent the person of God. But our Lord wished the inference to be drawn from this circumstance – concerning how far God, who is good and just, cares for those who supplicate him – that not even an unjust man can despise those who assail him with unceasing petitions, even were his motive merely to avoid annoyance (*Our Lord's Sermon on the Mount* 2:15:42).

In other words, if even an unjust judge will yield to repeated requests, how much more will the good and loving God respond when we persevere in prayer?

Persevering in prayer does not mean thinking that we must use many words to wear God down. Augustine also says:

[The Lord] has taught us to pray, not with much speaking, as if our being heard depended upon the fluency with which we express ourselves. He has taught us to pray recognising that we are praying to One who, as the Lord tells us, "knows what things we have need of before we ask him" (*Mt* 6:7-8). From this it may seem surprising that, although he has forbidden "much speaking," He who knows before we ask him what things we need has nevertheless given us exhortation to prayer in such words as these: "Men ought always to pray and not to faint" (*Lk* 18:1) (*Letters* 130:8:15).

The letter of James warns that sometimes our prayers are not fulfilled because we ask with wrong motives: "You ask and do not receive, because you ask wrongly, to spend it on your passions" (*Jm* 4:3).

The Church Fathers recognise our sins may pose a barrier to the fulfilment of prayer. But they add the consolation that when we purify our hearts and ask with sincerity, we may still receive what we ask. St Cyprian of Carthage states:

Let us ask, and we shall receive; and if there be delay and tardiness in our receiving, since we have grievously offended, let us knock, because "to him that knocks, it shall be opened" (*Lk* 11:10), if only our prayers, our groanings, and our tears, knock at the door; and with these we must be urgent and persevering (*Letters* 7:2).

Ultimately, God loves us and will give us the things we truly need (*Mt* 7:7-11).

Defending Life

"You shall not kill" is one of the Ten Commandments (*Ex* 20:13; *Dt* 5:17), and the *Book of Proverbs* exhorts us, "Rescue those who are being taken away to death; hold back those who are stumbling to the slaughter" (*Pr* 24:11).

Such exhortations are needed because our world is a violent place, and it always has been. In fact, the ancient world was even more violent, and the odds of dying a violent death were much higher.

Though we think of threats to life like abortion and assisted suicide as modern phenomena, they were present in the ancient world, particularly in pagan circles. Abortion and infanticide were well known, as was suicide. Sometimes people were pressured to kill themselves, or even legally required to do so by the state, and when they had trouble doing so, others would help them end their lives.

The early Christians recognised that all these practices were contrary to the Faith, that life is a gift from God, and that we cannot dispose of it at will.

Thus the first century Christian document known as the *Didache* condemns both abortion and infanticide, saying: "You shall not murder a child by abortion nor kill that which is begotten" (*Didache* 2).

In almost the same words, another first century document – the *Letter of Barnabas* – similarly condemns these practices: "Thou shalt not slay the child by procuring abortion; nor, again, shalt thou destroy it after it is born" (*Letter of Barnabas* 9).

These first century testimonies reveal how the pro-life ethic has been part of the Christian Faith from the very beginning.

Similarly, regarding suicide, the early Christian author Lactantius wrote:

> It was God who placed us in this abode of flesh. It was he who gave us the temporary dwelling of the body, that we should inhabit it as long as he pleased. Therefore it is to be considered wicked to wish to depart from it without the command of God. Therefore violence must not be applied to nature. He knows how to destroy his own work. And if any one shall apply wicked hands to that work, and shall tear asunder the bonds of the divine workmanship, he endeavours to flee from God, whose sentence no one will be able to escape, whether alive or dead. Therefore those who I have mentioned above are accursed and wicked, including those who have taught reasons to justify voluntary death. It was not enough for them to bear the guilt of being self-murderers, they even instructed others also in this wickedness (*Epitome of the Divine Institutes* 39).

Threats like abortion and suicide (assisted or otherwise) are still with us, and it is important that we defend the cause of life in our own day, always recognising and proclaiming the mercy that God has for those who have been involved in them (*CCC* 982, 2283).

Helping Those in Need

Helping those in need has been a Christian duty since the very beginning. Almsgiving is the first of the acts of piety Our Lord lists in Matthew 6 (the other two being prayer and fasting).

He urges his followers to give generously, that God may reward them in heaven, saying, "Sell your possessions, and give alms; provide yourselves with purses that do not grow old, with a treasure in the heavens that does not fail, where no thief approaches and no moth destroys" (*Lk* 12:33).

St Paul, similarly, says, "He who sows sparingly will also reap sparingly, and he who sows bountifully will also reap bountifully. Each one must do as he has made up his mind, not reluctantly or under compulsion, for God loves a cheerful giver" (2 *Co* 9:6-7).

At the same time, there is to be responsibility in giving. We have limited resources with which to help others, and we do not wish to enable destructive lifestyles (cf. 2 *Th* 3:6-15).

The same was true in the ancient world, when the vast majority of people lived in abject poverty. The balance between generosity and prudence is reflected in the first century Christian document known as the *Didache*. On the one hand, it stated: "Give to everyone that asks you, and ask it not back; for the Father wills that to all should be given of our own blessings (free gifts). Happy is he that gives according to the commandment; for he is guiltless" (*Didache* 1).

However, it also counsels prudence, saying: "But also now concerning this, it has been said, 'Let your alms sweat in your hands, until you know to whom you should give'" (ibid.).

While prudence is important, the accent is to be on generosity. Jesus identified himself with the poor, and he taught that when we feed and clothe the needy we are, in fact, feeding and clothing him (*Mt* 25:31-46). Thus St Jerome counselled the Roman widow Furia: "Consider the poor and needy. Give to everyone that asks of you, but especially unto them who are of the household of faith. Clothe the naked, feed the hungry, visit the sick. Every time that you hold out your hand, think of Christ" (*Letters* 54:12).

He also rebuked those who massed luxuries for themselves while ignoring the plight of the poor with whom Christ identified, saying:

Today you may see women cramming their wardrobes with dresses, changing their gowns from day to day, and for all that unable to vanquish the moths. Now and then one more scrupulous wears out a single dress; yet, while she appears in rags, her boxes are full. Parchments are dyed purple, gold is melted into lettering, manuscripts are decked with jewels, while Christ lies at the door, naked and dying (*Letters* 22:32).

God or Money?

We live in a materialistic culture. People today often focus on jobs, money, and possessions to the exclusion of God and spiritual values.

This is not new. Two thousand years ago, Jesus warned: "No one can serve two masters; for either he will hate the one and love the other, or he will be devoted to the one and despise the other. You cannot serve God and mammon" (*Mt* 6:24; cf. *Lk* 16:13).

Mammon is a loan word from Jesus's native language, Aramaic. It means "wealth" or "property." Jesus thus presents us with a choice between God and money. We can either make God our highest priority – or we can give into the temptation to treat money and the things it can buy as our highest priority.

To do that latter would make money our god. Thus St Paul warns: "Be sure of this, that no immoral or impure man, or one who is covetous (that is, an idolater), has any inheritance in the kingdom of Christ and of God" (*Ep* 5:5).

Later in the first century, an anonymous Christian author commented on how we can either serve the present material world or the future, spiritual world:

This world and the next are two enemies. The one urges us toward adultery and corruption, avarice, and deceit; the other bids farewell to these things. We cannot therefore be the friends of both; and it behooves us, by renouncing the one, to make sure of the other. Let us reckon that it is better to hate the things present, since they are trifling, transient, and corruptible; and to love those which are to come, as being good and incorruptible. For if we do the will of Christ, we shall find rest. Otherwise, nothing shall deliver us from eternal punishment, if we disobey his commandments (2 *Clement* 6).

In the mid-200s, Cyprian of Carthage wrote:

How can those follow Christ who are held back by the chain of their wealth? How can they seek heaven, and climb to sublime and lofty heights, if they are weighed down by earthly desires? They think that they possess things, when they are rather possessed by them. They are slaves of their profit – not lords with respect to their own money, but rather the bond-slaves of their money. These times and these men are indicated by the apostle, when he says, "those who desire to be rich fall into temptation, into a snare, into many senseless and hurtful desires that plunge men into ruin and destruction. For the love of money is the root of all evils; it is through this craving that some have wandered away from the faith and pierced their hearts with many pangs" (1 *Tm* 6:9-10) (*Treatise 3: On the Lapsed* 12).

The choice is therefore up to us. Who will we serve: God or money?

Fasting

In the Sermon on the Mount, Jesus gives us instructions about the spiritual practice of fasting. He expects this to be part of the Christian life, for he says *"when* you fast" (*Mt* 6:16), not *"if* you fast" (cf. *Mt* 9:14-15).

Our culture has almost totally forgotten the discipline of fasting. Today restaurants, markets, and food companies fill our lives with advertisements trying to tempt us to eat their wares. Sometimes they *literally* urge us to "give into temptation" and consume some delicacy they have for sale.

It is time we rediscovered the spiritual fast. Early Jews and Christians took fasting seriously. The pious Pharisee of Jesus's parable notes he fasted twice a week (*Lk* 18:12), and early Christians frequently fasted this often. The first century Church manual known as the *Didache* states: "But let not your fasts be with the hypocrites (*Mt* 6:16) for they fast on the second and fifth day of the week (Monday and Thursday); but fast on the fourth day and the day of Preparation (Wednesday and Friday)" (*Didache* 8).

Jesus also said we should not fast like the hypocrites, "for they disfigure their faces that their fasting may be seen by men. Truly, I say to you, they have received their reward. But when you fast, anoint your head and wash your face, that your fasting may not be seen by men but by your Father who is in secret; and your Father who sees in secret will reward you" (*Mt* 16:16-18).

St Hilary of Poitiers comments:

He [Jesus] teaches us that the benefit of fasting is gained without the outward display of a weakened body, and that we should not curry the favour of the pagans by a display of deprivation. Instead, every instance of fasting should have the beauty of a holy exercise.

For oil is the fruit of mercy according to the heavenly and prophetic word. Our head, that is, the rational part of our life, should be adorned with beautiful works because all understanding is in the head. Impurities on our face are washed off so that no one is appalled by its dishevelled appearance.

There is, however, a greater grace of [his] radiance in our encounter: once we are purified for the clarity of a good conscience and have been anointed with oil for the grace of works of mercy, our fasting commends us to God. Even when we shun the attention of others by fasting with our heads anointed, we will be more pleasing and be acknowledged (*Commentary on Matthew* 5:2).

While fasting should be part of the Christian life, we must also partake with thanks of the gifts God gives us, including food. "Let them thank the Lord for his steadfast love, for his wonderful works to the sons of men! For he satisfies him who is thirsty, and the hungry he fills with good things" (*Ps* 107:8-9).

Going to Church

Our culture is obsessed with individualism. We're constantly urged to "be yourself," to "have it your way," and to "look out for number one." While a healthy respect for the individual is essential, excessive focus on the self, by definition, is selfishness.

This attitude can affect our faith lives and isolate us from the Christian community. We can adopt a "Just me and Jesus" attitude, stop going to church, and arrogantly view our fellow Christians as unimportant to our lives.

But God wanted us to be a community. He founded a Church (*Mt* 16:18). He made us dependent on each other like the organs of a body (1 *Co* 12:12-27). And to properly live the Christian life, we need to go to church, "not neglecting to meet together, as is the habit of some" (*Heb* 10:25).

The Church Fathers recognised this. Just after AD 100, St Ignatius of Antioch wrote:

> Take heed, then, often to come together to give thanks to God, and show forth his praise. For when you assemble frequently in the same place, the powers of Satan are destroyed, and the destruction at which he aims is prevented by the unity of your faith. Nothing is more precious than peace, by which all war, both in heaven and earth, is brought to an end (*Epistle to the Ephesians* 13).

God made us social creatures (*Gn* 2:18; *Ps* 133:1), and we are not meant to be alone. Thus St John Chrysostom comments:

> In this we differ from beasts, for we have built cities, and markets, and houses, that we may be united one with another, not in the place of our dwelling only, but by the bond of love. Our nature came incomplete from him who made it, and it is not self-sufficient. Therefore, God, for our advantage, ordained that the needs we have from this should be filled by the assistance that comes from mutual interaction; so that what was lacking in one should be supplied by another (*Homilies on the Gospel of John* 19:1).

He also comments on how our spiritual lives are strengthened and how we avoid sin by contact with other committed Christians: "For nothing so especially makes persons easily vanquished and subdued in temptations, as isolation. For, tell me, if you scatter a phalanx in war, the enemy will have no trouble but will take them prisoners, coming on them separately and thereby all the more helpless" (*Homilies on the Epistle to the Hebrews* 30:2).

It is only by gathering together as Christians, to hear the Word of God proclaimed and to receive the sacraments, that our souls are satisfied. And it is only when we are drawn out of ourselves and interact with our fellow Christians that we can help others in love and receive their love and help in return.

Our Spiritual Gifts

God did not mean for us to live the Christian life in isolation. He established a Church (*Mt* 16:18), and he wants us both to help each other and to receive help from each other. He wants to draw us out of ourselves and build up the Christian community in love. Others have needs that we can fill, and we have needs that others can fill.

To this end, the Holy Spirit has given each of us spiritual gifts that we can – and must – use to serve our fellow members of the body of Christ. St Paul discusses the theme of spiritual gifts on a number of occasions (cf. *Rm* 12:3-13; 1 *Co* 12:1-14:40; *Ep* 4:11-14).

Our gifts are not all the same. Sometimes God gives people obviously supernatural gifts like prophecy, speaking in tongues, or performing miracles of healing (*Rm* 12:6; 1 *Co* 12:10). However, most of the time God gives people gifts that are less-obviously supernatural, such as the ability to serve others, to teach the Faith, to contribute to their needs, to perform acts of mercy (*Rm* 12:7-8).

We do not need to worry if we have been given less spectacular gifts (1 *Co* 12:14-26). We should rejoice that we have been given a way of serving our fellow Christians and building up the body of Christ.

The Church Fathers recognised the importance of the mutual contributions we make by exercising our spiritual gifts. Thus St Augustine said:

This man has one gift, that man another; and what that man has, this man has not. There is a measure, a certain division of gifts. Therefore, [the Holy Spirit] is given to men by measure, and concord among them makes one body. As the hand receives one kind of gift to work, [and] the eye another to see...so are also the gifts of believers diverse, distributed to them as to members, to each according to his proper measure (*Tractates on the Gospel of John* 14:10).

Whatever our spiritual gifts, we must remember that they – like all the graces of the Christian life – are things we receive from God for the benefit of others, not things we should flatter ourselves about. As St John Chrysostom said:

For these excellent things do not belong to you, but to the grace of God. If you name faith, it came of his calling; or if you speak of the forgiveness of sins, or spiritual gifts, or the word of teaching, or miracles; you received all from that origin. Now what do you have, tell me, which you have not received but have rather achieved by your own self? You have nothing to say. Well, you have received. Should that make you high-minded? No, it ought to make you shrink back into yourself. For what has been given is not yours but the Giver's (*Homilies on 1 Corinthians* 12:3).

Our Shepherds in Christ

Today people resist anybody telling them what to do or think. Even many Christians have a "just me and Jesus" attitude which dismisses the role of the Church and its leaders.

Yet Christ gave his ministers the authority to teach, telling them: "He who hears you hears me, and he who rejects you rejects me, and he who rejects me rejects him who sent me" (*Lk* 10:16).

Similarly, the author of Hebrews tells us: "Obey your leaders and submit to them; for they are keeping watch over your souls, as men who will have to give account. Let them do this joyfully, and not sadly, for that would be of no advantage to you" (*Heb* 13:17; cf. 1 *Th* 5:12-13).

Early Christians recognised the authority that Christ had given the leaders of his Church, and we find the same kind of exhortations in the writings of the Church Fathers.

At the dawn of the second century, St Ignatius of Antioch told his readers of the importance of respecting their bishop: "We ought to receive every one whom the Master of the house sends to be over his household, as we would do him that sent him. It is clear, therefore, that we should look upon the bishop even as we would upon the Lord himself" (*Letter to the Ephesians* 6).

He also warned against respecting the bishop with one's lips but ignoring his authority:

It is fitting, then, not only to be called Christians, but to be so in reality, for some indeed give one the title of bishop, but do all things without him. Now such persons seem to me to be not possessed of a good conscience, seeing that they are not steadfastly gathered together according to the commandment (*Letter to the Magnesians* 4).

Priests and deacons are also owed respect. St Ignatius wrote: "Give heed to the bishop, that God also may give heed to you. I offer up my soul for those that are submissive to the bishop, to the presbyters, and to the deacons, and may my portion be along with them in God!" (*Letter to Polycarp* 6).

God has instituted the leaders of his Church not so that they might lord it over us but so that they might serve us spiritually and bring us closer to Christ (*Mk* 10:42-45). Thus the St Augustine commented on the times he and his fellow leaders experience joy in their ministry:

When do we do it with joy? When we see a man making progress in the words of God. When does the labourer in the field work with joy? When he looks at the tree and sees the fruit; when he looks at the crop and sees the prospect of an abundance of grain on the threshing floor; when he sees that he has not laboured in vain, has not bowed his back, and bruised his hands and endured the cold and heat in vain (*Sermons* 32:15[82:12]).

Avoiding False Teachers

We must guard our Christian Faith for the precious gift that it is and not allow it to be corrupted by false teaching – even when that teaching comes from those who identify themselves as Christians.

Jesus commanded us: "Beware of false prophets, who come to you in sheep's clothing but inwardly are ravenous wolves" (*Mt* 7:15).

Similarly, St Peter warned: "There will be false teachers among you, who will secretly bring in destructive heresies, even denying the Master who bought them, bringing upon themselves swift destruction" (2 *P* 2:1).

The early Christians – who had to confront many heresies – were well aware of this danger and took it with deadly earnestness. At the dawn of the second century, St Ignatius of Antioch told his readers:

> Some are in the habit of carrying about the name [of Jesus Christ] with wicked cunning, practising things unworthy of God. You must flee them as you would wild beasts. For they are ravening dogs, who bite secretly. Against them you must be on your guard, inasmuch as they are men who can scarcely be cured (*Letter to the Ephesians* 7).

He also complimented his readers for resisting those preaching false doctrines:

> I have heard of some who have visited you with false doctrine. You did not allow them to sow it among

you, but stopped your ears, that you might not receive the things which they sowed. [You acted] like stones belonging to the temple of the Father, prepared for the building of God the Father, and drawn up on high by the instrument of Jesus Christ, which is the cross (cf. 1 *P* 2:5), making use of the Holy Spirit as a rope. Your faith was the means by which you ascended, and your love the way which led up to God (ibid. 9).

Finally, he warned of the fate that awaited both false teachers and those who followed them:

Do not err, my brethren. Those that corrupt families shall not inherit the kingdom of God. If, then, those who do this in respect to the flesh have suffered death, how much more shall this be the case with anyone who corrupts by wicked doctrine the faith of God, for which Jesus Christ was crucified! A person becoming defiled [in this way], shall go away into everlasting fire, and so shall every one that listens unto him (ibid. 16).

Unfortunately, the list of heresies that the Church has faced is not short. There have always been those in the Christian community who have spread false teachings – from the Judaisers who St Paul battled in the first century to the Gnostics of the second and third centuries, from the Arians and Pneumatomachians of the fourth century, and from countless others down to our own day.

The good news is that we may always trust in the teaching of the Church "the pillar and bulwark of the truth" (1 *Tm* 3:15).

Chastity

Our society makes it difficult to live a life of chastity. We live in an age of loose sexual morals, and we are constantly bombarded with temptations. The Internet has made pornography just a click away and "hook-ups" just a swipe away.

Yet temptations to sexual impurity are not new. "You shall not commit adultery" and "You shall not covet your neighbour's wife" are found in the Ten Commandments (*Ex* 20:14, 17). Jesus warned that to deliberately gaze on a woman to foster lust is to commit adultery in your heart (*Mt* 5:28). And St Paul warned, "Do not be deceived; neither the immoral, nor idolaters, nor adulterers, nor sexual perverts, nor thieves, nor the greedy, nor drunkards, nor revilers, nor robbers will inherit the kingdom of God" (1 *Co* 6:9-10).

The early Christians recognised the seriousness of sexual sin. The first century Christian author Hermas received a vision in which he was given a warning by his guardian angel:

> "I charge you," he said, "to guard your chastity, and let no thought enter your heart of another man's wife, or of fornication, or of similar iniquities. If you do, you will commit a great sin. But if you always remember your own wife, you will never sin. For if [an adulterous] thought enters your heart, then you will sin; and if, in like manner, you think other wicked

thoughts, you commit sin. For this [kind of] thought is great sin in a servant of God, and if any one commit this wicked deed, he works death for himself" (*The Shepherd* 2:4:1).

The need to avoid sexual sin has been recognised by Christians from the first century through today. It is a key part of the Christian message.

The good news is that God has the power to liberate us from sexual sins. After affirming that those who deliberately indulge in sexual sin will not inherit the kingdom, St Paul continued: "And such were some of you. But you were washed, you were sanctified, you were justified in the name of the Lord Jesus Christ and in the Spirit of our God" (1 *Co* 6:11).

He also provided this word of hope and comfort: "No temptation has overtaken you that is not common to man. God is faithful, and he will not let you be tempted beyond your strength, but with the temptation will also provide the way of escape, that you may be able to endure it" (1 *Co* 10:13).

How can we find that way of escape? By focusing not on our temptations but on what is good: "Brethren, whatever is true, whatever is honourable, whatever is just, whatever is pure, whatever is lovely, whatever is gracious, if there is any excellence, if there is anything worthy of praise, think about these things" (*Ph* 4:8).

The Religious Life

Since ancient times, some people have been called to lead lives of special consecration to God. In the Old Testament, people could make themselves consecrated (Hebrew, *nazir*), either temporarily or permanently, by taking the Nazirite vow (*Nb* 6:2-21).

In the Christian age, Jesus recommended consecration to God by the discipline of celibacy, stating:

> "Not all men can receive this saying, but only those to whom it is given. For there are eunuchs who have been so from birth, and there are eunuchs who have been made eunuchs by men, and there are eunuchs who have made themselves eunuchs for the sake of the kingdom of heaven. He who is able to receive this, let him receive it" (Mt 19:11-12).

St Paul similarly spoke of a first century order of widows (1 *Tm* 5:3-16), who also pledged celibacy (1 *Tm* 5:11-12). Today there are many religious orders where men and women live the evangelical counsels of poverty, chastity, and obedience.

Living a life of special consecration to God via vows is not a new development but something that has existed all through Church history, as illustrated both by the New Testament and the writings of the Church Fathers.

One of the most influential early monks was St Anthony of Egypt (c. AD 251-356), who is known as the father of monasticism. In addition to men who remained unmarried that they might serve Christ with an undivided heart (cf. 1 *Co* 7:32-35), many women also became consecrated virgins. Thus St Patrick rejoiced over how in his day both men and women were embracing the consecrated life:

Behold, how the Irish who never had the knowledge of God, and hitherto worshipped only idols and unclean things, have lately become the people of the Lord, and are called the sons of God.

The sons and daughters of Scottish princes are monks and virgins of Christ. And there was one blessed Scottish maiden, very fair, of noble birth, and of adult age, whom I baptised, and after a few days she came to me, because, as she declared, she had received a response from a messenger of God, desiring her to become a virgin of Christ, and to draw near to God. Thanks be to God, on the sixth day after that, she with most praiseworthy eagerness, entered that state of life which all the virgins of God likewise now adopt, not with the permission of their parents. No, they endure persecution and unfounded reproaches from their parents, and nevertheless the number increases the more; and as to those of our kind who are born [of God] there, we know not the number, except widows and continent persons. But those [virgins] who are detained in slavery are the most severely afflicted, yet they persevere in spite of terrors and threats (*Confession* 17-18[41-42]).

Showing Off How Spiritual We Are

We all have a tendency to show off our positive qualities, and that – unfortunately – includes our spirituality. We must fight this tendency. Jesus tells us, "Beware of practising your piety before men in order to be seen by them; for then you will have no reward from your Father who is in heaven" (*Mt* 6:1). And he excoriates the Pharisees, who "do all their deeds to be seen by men; for they make their phylacteries broad and their fringes long, and they love the place of honour at feasts and the best seats in the synagogues, and salutations in the market places, and being called rabbi by men" (*Mt* 23:5-7).

Instead, he says, we should do our good deeds in secret, so that they will not be seen by men "but by your Father who is in secret; and your Father who sees in secret will reward you" (*Mt* 6:17; cf. vv. 4, 6). On the other hand, he also says, "Let your light so shine before men, that they may see your good works and give glory to your Father who is in heaven" (*Mt* 5:16).

The point is that we must do good for the right motive: to please God, not to bring glory to ourselves. To the extent we can, we should do good works in a way that brings public glory to God, but when the temptation is to glorify ourselves, we should do them discreetly.

The Church Fathers recognised the temptation to show off spiritually. The early Christian writer Origen commented:

[Evil thoughts sometimes] make worthy of censure even those things which seem good, and which, so far as the judgement of the masses is concerned, are worthy of praise. Accordingly, if we do alms before men, having in our thoughts the intent to appear philanthropic to men, and of being honoured because of this philanthropy, we receive our reward only from men. And, universally, everything that is done with the consciousness in the one who does it that he will be glorified by men, has no reward from him who beholds in secret, and renders in secret the reward to those who are pure (*Commentary on Matthew* 10:15).

The temptation to flaunt one's spirituality is always with us, and St Jerome commented on how he witnessed people indulging in it in his own day, even in St Peter's Basilica in Rome:

When they hold out a hand to the needy, they sound a trumpet. When they invite people to an *agape* meal, they engage a crier. I lately saw the noblest lady in Rome – I suppress her name, for I am no satirist – with a band of eunuchs before her in the basilica of the blessed Peter. She was giving money to the poor, a coin apiece; and this with her own hand, that she might be accounted more religious (*Letters* 22:32).

Dealing with Anxieties and Fears

All of us have fear in our lives. It is part of the human condition. But Jesus urges us to deal with our daily worries by seeking to please God and having confidence in him, for he can provide for our every need. He says:

> "Therefore do not be anxious, saying, 'What shall we eat?' or 'What shall we drink?' or 'What shall we wear?' For the Gentiles seek all these things; and your heavenly Father knows that you need them all. But seek first his kingdom and his righteousness, and all these things shall be yours as well. Therefore do not be anxious about tomorrow, for tomorrow will be anxious for itself" (*Mt* 6:31-33).

Life in the age of the Church Fathers was insecure, and most people lived in abject poverty. These words thus had special meaning for them, but they also apply to us. Clement of Alexandria explains:

> To those, therefore, that have made progress in the word, he has proclaimed this utterance, bidding them dismiss anxious care concerning the things of this world, and exhorting them to rely on the Father alone, in imitation of children. As a result, in what follows he also says: "Do not be anxious about tomorrow, for tomorrow will be anxious for itself. Let the day's own trouble be sufficient for the day" (*Mt* 6:34). Thus he instructs them to lay aside the cares of this life, and

36

depend on the Father alone. And he who fulfils this commandment is in reality a child and a son to God (*The Instructor* 1:5).

Our Lord does not mean we should not reasonably plan for the future or work to procure the things we need (2 *Th* 3:10), but it does mean that we should not allow our worldly cares to consume us and cause us to lose focus on pleasing God.

He also does not mean that will never have troubles. Experience shows it is God's will to allow us to encounter difficulties in life. St Augustine explains:

This entire precept is reduced, therefore, to the following rule: namely, that even in the procuring of these things we should keep our mind on the kingdom of God, and that in the service of the kingdom of God we should give no thought to these things. In this way, even if these things be lacking at times (and God permits this usually for the sake of exercising us), not only do they not weaken our resolve, but they even strengthen it (*Commentary on the Lord's Sermon on the Mount* 2:17:58).

Thus we should not dwell on future troubles but keep our focus on God. "Cast all your anxieties on him, for he cares about you" (1 *P* 5:7).

When Others Wrong Us

Sometimes in life people wrong us. They may injure us – physically, emotionally, or spiritually. They may harm our reputation. They may steal from us. They may even betray us.

In the Sermon on the Mount, Jesus tells us, "if any one strikes you on the right cheek, turn to him the other also; and if anyone would sue you and take your coat, let him have your cloak as well; and if any one forces you to go one mile, go with him two miles" (*Mt* 5:39-41). Here Jesus exhorts us to have a loving and generous attitude, even toward those who harm us. As he also says, "Love your enemies and pray for those who persecute you" (*Mt* 5:44).

Arnobius of Sicca comments on how the loving attitude of Christians helped calm violent tendencies in the ancient world:

> For since we [Christians] – a numerous band of men as we are – have learned from his teaching and his laws that evil ought not to be repaid with evil, that it is better to suffer wrong than to inflict it, and that we should rather shed our own blood than stain our hands and our conscience with that of another, an ungrateful world is now for a long period enjoying a benefit from Christ. For by his means the rage of savage ferocity has been softened and has begun to withhold hostile hands from the blood of a fellow creature (*Against the Heathen* 1:6).

In commanding us to have a loving attitude, Jesus did not mean for us to excuse or ignore sin. Thus he also gave instructions for correcting a brother who sins against us, saying that we should approach him first privately, then bring in others if needed, and finally turn the matter over to the Church (*Mt* 18:15-17). He thus counselled us to use the most modest means necessary to deal with the problem, and not to start by going behind another's back or over his head.

This is, after all, how we ourselves want to be treated. Thus Theodoret of Cyr wrote to a man he had offended:

> I do not know what offence I can have given to your Excellency. We err unwillingly as well as willingly, and sometimes are quite ignorant in what way we are transgressing. I therefore beg your greatness – remembering the divine laws which plainly charge us, "If your brother sins against you, go and tell him his fault, between you and him alone" (*Mt* 18:15) – to make plain to me the origin of the annoyance, that I may either prove myself innocent, or, made aware of where I was wrong, may beg your pardon (*Letter 96*).

By taking a loving attitude when we are wronged and trying to settle the matter privately, we thus fulfil the Golden Rule: "So whatever you wish that men would do to you, do so to them" (*Mt* 7:12).

Forgiving Others

Jesus makes it very clear that we must be willing to forgive others, telling us: "If your brother sins, rebuke him, and if he repents, forgive him; and if he sins against you seven times in the day, and turns to you seven times, and says, 'I repent,' you must forgive him" (*Lk* 17:3-4).

Being willing to forgive others is a frequent theme in Jesus's teachings, and the Church Fathers recognised how important it was. Pope St Clement I wrote:

> Let us therefore, brethren, be of humble mind, laying aside all haughtiness, and pride, and foolishness, and angry feelings; and let us act according to that which is written...being especially mindful of the words of the Lord Jesus which he spake, teaching us meekness and long-suffering. For thus he spoke: "Be ye merciful, that ye may obtain mercy; forgive, that it may be forgiven to you; as ye do, so shall it be done unto you; as ye judge, so shall ye be judged; as ye are kind, so shall kindness be shown to you; with what measure ye mete, with the same it shall be measured to you" (cf. *Mt* 6:12-15, 7:2; *Lk* 6:36-38). By this precept and by these rules let us stablish ourselves, that we walk with all humility in obedience to his holy words (*Letter to the Corinthians* 13).

When we forgive others, it does not mean that there are no consequences for what they have done to us. "It is not in our power not to feel or to forget an offense; but the heart that offers itself to the Holy Spirit turns injury into compassion and purifies the memory in transforming the hurt into intercession" (*CCC* 2843).

Forgiving others also does not mean that it is a sin to be angry with someone. But it does mean not dwelling on our anger and being willing to let it go. St Paul says: "Be angry but do not sin; do not let the sun go down on your anger" (*Ep* 4:26).

In the same way, Lactantius wrote:

Patience is to be regarded as a very great virtue; and that the just man might obtain this, God willed, as has been before said, that he should be despised as sluggish. For unless he shall have been insulted, it will not be known what fortitude he has in restraining himself... Therefore, since it is impossible and useless to resist nature, so that we are not excited at all; before, however, the emotion bursts forth to the infliction of injury, as far as is possible let it be calmed in time. God has enjoined us not to let the sun go down upon our wrath (*Divine Institutes* 6:18).

Taking Up Our Cross

Jesus provides the model of the Christian life. He is the example which we must imitate. This includes his example of being willing to suffer to do what is right and fulfil God's will.

Jesus went to the cross knowing that this was God's will for him and that it was how God would bring about the redemption of the world. In the same way, Jesus expects us to carry the crosses that enter our own lives.

He told us:

> "If any man would come after me, let him deny himself and take up his cross daily and follow me. For whoever would save his life will lose it; and whoever loses his life for my sake, he will save it. For what does it profit a man if he gains the whole world and loses or forfeits himself?" (*Lk* 9:23-25; cf. *Mt* 10:38, 16:24).

All of us face challenges in life, and we must make choices in how to deal with them. If we deal with them in a patient, faithful manner, God will bless us. "Blessed is the man who endures trial, for when he has stood the test he will receive the crown of life which God has promised to those who love him" (*Jm* 1:12).

However, we can be tempted to betray our Christian principles. Our culture has become hostile to the Faith, and it constantly presents us with challenges. We must remain strong and overcome these. "To him who conquers I will grant to eat of the tree of life, which is in the paradise of God" (*Rv* 2:7).

For inspiration in dealing with the challenges of our day, we may turn to the Church Fathers, who faced even greater persecution. Some of them *literally* shouldered crosses and died martyrs' deaths.

During the age of persecution, St Cyprian of Carthage received a letter from a number of confessors – people who professed the Christian Faith despite persecution. Commenting on passages like the ones we have quoted, they wrote:

> When we read these things, and things of the same kind, brought together in the Gospel, and feel, as it were, torches placed under us, with the Lord's words to inflame our faith, we not only do not dread, but we even provoke the enemies of the truth. And we have already conquered the opponents of God, by the very fact of our not yielding to them, and we have subdued their nefarious laws against the truth. And although we have not yet shed our blood, we are prepared to shed it (Cyprian, *Letters* 25:5).

These confessors were just a few of the countless Christians who faced intense persecution in the early days of the Church. If they remained true to the Faith and refused to deny their principles, we can be confident that God will give us the strength to do so as well.

When We Have Fallen

As long as we are in this life, we must struggle with our sinful, fallen nature. "If we say we have no sin, we deceive ourselves, and the truth is not in us" (1 *Jn* 1:8). However, the good news is that God is always willing to forgive us when we repent and go to confession. "If we confess our sins, he is faithful and just, and will forgive our sins and cleanse us from all unrighteousness" (1 *Jn* 1:9).

We all commit venial sins, and these can be forgiven apart from the sacrament of confession. However, when we have committed mortal sin we must go to confession and perform our penance. St Augustine explained to his catechumens:

> When you have been baptised, hold fast to a good life in the commandments of God, that you may guard your baptism even to the end. I do not tell you that you will live here without sin; but they are venial sins, of which this life is not free. For the sake of all sins baptism was provided; for the sake of light sins, which we cannot be without, prayer was provided. What does the [Lord's] Prayer say? "Forgive us our debts, as we also forgive our debtors" (*Mt* 6:12). Once for all we have washing in baptism; every day we have washing in prayer. Only, do not commit those things for which you must be separated from Christ's body. Far be those from you! For those whom you have seen doing penance, who have committed heinous things, either

adulteries or other enormous crimes – for these they do penance. Because if theirs had been light sins, daily prayer would suffice to blot these out... In three ways, then, are sins remitted in the Church: by baptism, by prayer, and by the greater humility of penance (*Sermon to Catechumens on the Creed* 15, 16).

St Paul warns against receiving the Eucharist in an unworthy manner (1 *Co* 11:27-28), and the early Christians recognised that, if we have committed mortal sin, we need confession (which in their day was often made publicly) before receiving the Eucharist. The first century document known as the *Didache* states: "Every Lord's day gather yourselves together and break bread and give thanksgiving, after having confessed your transgressions, that your sacrifice may be pure" (*Didache* 14).

Sometimes people are afraid to confess their sins, but it is vital that they do so. St Jerome explains:

If the serpent, the devil, bites someone secretly, he infects that person with the venom of sin. And if the one who has been bitten keeps silence and does not do penance, and does not want to confess his wound... then his brother and his master, who have the word [of absolution] that will cure him, cannot very well assist him (*Commentary on Ecclesiastes* 10:11).

The Death of Our Loved Ones

Sooner or later, all of us lose loved ones – grandparents, parents, friends. Some of us, most tragically, even lose children. But from a Christian perspective, death is not the end, and we will see our loved ones again.

St Paul tells us: "We would not have you ignorant, brethren, concerning those who are asleep, that you may not grieve as others do who have no hope. For since we believe that Jesus died and rose again, even so, through Jesus, God will bring with him those who have fallen asleep" (1 *Th* 4:13-14).

He goes on to describe how, at the end of the world (not before), Jesus will raise the dead and gather all believers to be with him forever in an eternal communion of love (1 *Th* 4:15-18).

The early Christians shared this hope. In AD 252, St Cyprian of Carthage wrote:

We who live in hope, believe in God, and trust that Christ suffered for us and rose again – abiding in Christ and rising again through him and in him – why either are we ourselves unwilling to depart from this life, or why do we bewail and grieve for our friends when they depart, as if they were lost. Christ himself, our Lord and God, encourages us and says, "I am the resurrection and the life; he who believes in me, though he die, yet shall he live, and whoever lives and believes in me shall never die." (*Jn* 11:25-26). If we believe in

Christ, let us have faith in his words and promises. And since we shall not die eternally, let us come with a glad security to Christ, with whom we are both to conquer and to reign for ever (*On Mortality* 21).

St John Chrysostom similarly wrote that, while it is natural for us to mourn our loved ones, our grief should be tempered by hope:

> If we see any one sleeping, we are not disturbed or distressed, expecting that he will certainly get up. Even so, when we see any one dead, let us not be disturbed or dejected, for this also is a sleep – a longer one indeed, but still a sleep. By giving it the name of slumber [Paul] comforted the mourners and overthrew the accusation of the unbelievers. If you mourn immoderately over him who has departed, you will be like that unbeliever who has no hope of a resurrection. He, indeed, does well to mourn, inasmuch as he cannot exercise any spiritual wisdom concerning things to come. But you who have received such strong proofs concerning the future life, why do you sink into the same weakness with him? (*Homily on the Paralytic Let Down Through the Roof* 8).

We thus live in the hope of being united with Christ and our loved ones for eternity, and therefore are to "comfort one another with these words" (1 *Th* 4:18).

Helping Our Departed Loved Ones

Sooner or later, death separates us from those we love. In light of our Christian Faith, St Paul tells us not to grieve like those who have no hope (1 *Th* 4:13).

However, death does not separate us in a way that prevents us helping those whom we love. We can still pray for them and ask God to give them rest and comfort while they await the resurrection of the dead. This is something Jews and Christians have done since before the time of Christ.

When Judah Maccabee and his men found the bodies of comrades who had fallen in battle, they prayed that they might be freed from the consequences of their sins. They also took up a collection so that a sacrifice might be offered at the temple in Jerusalem – the ancient equivalent of having Mass said for someone (2 *M* 12:38-46).

In the New Testament, St Paul prays that God will show mercy on the last day to a man named Onesiphorous, who apparently had died, as Paul speaks of him only in the past tense (2 *Tm* 1:16-18).

Early Christian inscriptions bear witness to the belief that the living can pray for the departed. In his epitaph, a second century Christian calling himself "Agape" (Greek, *love, charity*) wrote: "I pray you, O brethren, to pray when you come here, and to ask the Father and the Son in your common prayers. May it be in your minds to remember dear Agape, that the omnipotent God may keep Agape safe forever" (*Christian Inscriptions* no. 34).

Around AD 190, a Christian named Abercius had an epitaph carved for him in which he said: "These things I, Abercius, commanded to be written when I was on earth; and truly, I was seventy two years old. Let him who understands this, and everyone who agrees with it, pray for Abercius" (*Christian Inscriptions*, no. 43).

A little after the year 200, Tertullian of Carthage wrote:

> A woman, after the death of her husband...prays for his soul and asks that he may, while waiting [the resurrection of the dead], find rest – and that he may share in the first resurrection (cf. *Rv* 20:6). And each year, on the anniversary of his death, she offers the [Eucharistic] sacrifice for him (*Monogamy* 10).

And St Augustine wrote:

> During the time, moreover, that intervenes between a man's death and the final resurrection, the soul dwells in a hidden retreat, where it enjoys rest or suffers affliction in proportion to the reward it earned by the life it led on earth. Nor can it be denied that the souls of the dead are benefited by the piety of their living friends, who offer the sacrifice of the Mediator, or give alms in the church on their behalf (*Enchiridion on Faith, Hope, and Charity* 109-110).

Seeking Help from the Saints

Scripture reveals that the saints in heaven pray for us. Thus Judah Maccabee was given a vision of the high priest Onias and the prophet Jeremiah, both of whom were deceased, praying for all the Jewish people (2 *M* 15:12-14). In the New Testament, we see the saints and angels in heaven offering to God the prayers of the saints on earth in the form of incense (*Rv* 5:8, 8:3-4).

It has only been natural, therefore, for Christians to ask the saints and angels to be our partners in prayer and to intercede with God alongside us.

Thus on early Christian gravestones we find inscriptions to deceased loved ones, asking for their prayers, such as this one from Rome in the 300s: "Atticus, sleep in peace, secure in your safety, and pray anxiously for our sins" (*Christian Inscriptions*, no. 37).

St Gregory of Nazianz explained why we would want those in heaven, in particular, to pray for us, saying:

> Yes, I am well assured that [my father's] intercession is of more avail now than his instruction was in former days – for he is closer to God, now that he has shaken off his bodily fetters, has freed his mind from the clay that obscured it, and holds conversation naked with the nakedness of the prime and purest Mind (*Orations* 18:4).

Similarly, St Jerome writes: "If apostles and martyrs can pray for others while still in the body – when they still ought to be anxious for themselves – how much more must they do so when once they have won their crowns, overcome, and triumphed?" (*Against Vigilantius* 6).

The invocation of the saints also found its place in the Church's liturgy. St Cyril of Jerusalem explains: "[During the Eucharistic Prayer] we commemorate those who have already fallen asleep: first, the patriarchs, prophets, apostles, and martyrs, that in their prayers and supplications God would receive our petition" (*Catechetical Lectures* 23:9).

And St John Chrysostom records how even noble Christians humble themselves by making special visits to the tombs of the saints to ask for their intercession:

> He who wears the purple [of nobility] himself goes to embrace those tombs, and, laying aside his pride, stands begging the saints to be his advocates with God. And he that wears the crown [of royalty] implores the tentmaker [St Paul] and the fisherman [St Peter], though dead, to be his patrons (*Homilies on Second Corinthians* 26:2:5).

Christian devotion to the saints not only involves asking for their intercession but also learning from their example. St Augustine explains: "It is true that Christians pay religious honour to the memory of the martyrs, both to motivate us to imitate them and to obtain a share in their rewards and to obtain the assistance of their prayers" (*Reply to Faustus the Manichean* 20:21 [c. AD 400]).

Devotion to the Blessed Mother

From the very beginning, Christians have had special regard for the Mother of Our Lord. The Blessed Virgin herself proclaimed that, "Henceforth all generations will call me blessed; for he who is mighty has done great things for me" (*Lk* 1:48-49). Down through the ages, this recognition has taken many forms and resulted in many kinds of Marian devotion.

All of these are rooted in the grace that God showed Mary. St Jerome comments: "Observe: She says she is blessed not by her own merit and virtue, but by the mercy of God dwelling in her" (*Against the Pelagians* 1:16).

Early Christians recognised that, by God's grace, Mary had been given a unique role in his plan of the ages. Mankind was originally plunged into sin by Adam, whose work was facilitated by Eve (*Gn* 3:6). Jesus was the Second Adam, who rescued man from sin, and his work was facilitated by Mary, who agreed to become his mother (*Lk* 1:38). The Church Fathers thus saw Mary as the Second Eve. In the mid-100s, St Justin Martyr wrote:

> [The Son of God] became man by the Virgin so that the disobedience which proceeded from the serpent might be destroyed in the same manner it derived its origin. For Eve, who was a virgin and undefiled, having conceived the serpent's word [in her mind], brought forth disobedience and death. But the Virgin Mary received faith and joy, when the angel Gabriel

announced the good tidings to her that the Spirit of the Lord would come upon her and the power of the Most High would overshadow her (*Dialogue with Trypho* 100).

St Jerome summarised this by saying, "Death came through Eve, but life has come through Mary" (*Letters* 22:21).

Christians naturally turned to Mary and asked for her intercession. An early version of the prayer now known as the *Sub Tuum Praesidium* (Latin, "Under Your Protection") is found on a Greek manuscript that may date as early as AD 250: "Mother of God, [hear] my petitions. Do not disregard us in adversity, but rescue us from danger" (*Rylands Papyrus* 470).

Similarly the anonymous author of an ancient *Oration on Simeon and Anna* invokes the Virgin and asks her to remember Christians in her prayers:

Hail to you for ever, virgin mother of God, our unceasing joy, for I again return to you. You are the beginning of our feast; you are its middle and end; the pearl of great price that belongs to the kingdom... [You brought forth] the invisible Son of the Father – the Prince of Peace – who in a marvellous manner manifested himself as less than all littleness. Therefore, we pray you, most excellent among women – who boasts in the confidence of your maternal honours – that you would unceasingly keep us in remembrance (Ch. 14).

Our Own Death

Death comes to us all. It is a fact of life, and it is natural to fear death. God meant us to value our earthly lives, and he made us so that we fear the evil of death and thus seek to preserve our lives.

Even Jesus experienced aversion to the thought of his death. As the Crucifixion approached, he told his disciples, "My soul is very sorrowful, even to death" (*Mt* 26:38). Yet he was willing to accept his death, telling his Father, "Not as I will, but as you will" (*Mt* 26:39).

In this, he sets the example we must follow. We can and should avoid death – by staying out of danger, preserving our health, and seeking medical treatment. But when it becomes clear that it is our time to die, we must accept it as God's will.

Yet we do so in hope, for as Christians we have the hope of the resurrection. St Paul compares our bodies to seeds that are sown in the ground, only to sprout forth in a new and glorious plant (1 *Co* 15:36-37). What is more, our new life in our resurrected bodies will be far better than this one, for "What is sown is perishable, what is raised is imperishable" (1 *Co* 15:42), and Christ "will change our lowly body to be like his glorious body" (*Ph* 3:21).

The early Christians also shared this view. In AD 252, St Cyprian of Carthage wrote:

[When] we die, we are passing over to immortality by death. Nor can eternal life follow, unless it we depart from this life. It is not an ending, but a transit, and – this journey of time being completed – a passage to eternity. Who would not hasten to better things? Who would not crave to be changed and renewed into the likeness of Christ and to arrive more quickly at the dignity of heavenly glory? For Paul the apostle says, "For our commonwealth is in heaven, and from it we await a Saviour, the Lord Jesus Christ, who will change our lowly body to be like his glorious body" (*Ph* 3:20-21).

Christ the Lord also promises that we shall be such, when...he prays to the Father for us, saying, "Father, I desire that they also, whom you have given me, may be with me where I am, to behold my glory which you have given me in your love for me before the foundation of the world" (*Jn* 17:24). One who is to attain to the throne of Christ, to the glory of the heavenly kingdoms, ought not to mourn nor lament, but rather, in accordance with the Lord's promise, in accordance with his faith in the truth, he ought to rejoice in this his departure and translation (*On Mortality* 22).

Treasure in Heaven

God must be our fundamental priority in life. Jesus taught us:

"Do not lay up for yourselves treasures on earth, where moth and rust consume and where thieves break in and steal, but lay up for yourselves treasures in heaven, where neither moth nor rust consumes and where thieves do not break in and steal. For where your treasure is, there will your heart be also" (*Mt* 6:19-21).

In this life we all have things of value, and we are naturally concerned about protecting them. None of us would want to lose our wallets or our phones, and we would be mortified if someone cleaned out our bank accounts or burned down our houses.

Yet all the things of this life will pass, and what will we have then? Only the treasures we have laid up in heaven. Keeping that fact in focus in this life will help us keep our priorities in order.

Concerning Jesus's instruction to lay up treasure in heaven, St Augustine writes:

Those who have listened to this injunction have proved in the time of trouble how well they were advised not to despise this most trustworthy Teacher, and most faithful and mighty Guardian of their treasure. For if many were glad that their treasure was stored in places which the enemy happened not to discover, how much better founded was the joy of those who, by the counsel of their God, had fled with their treasure to a citadel which no enemy can possibly reach! (*City of God* 1:10:2).

We lay up treasure in heaven by doing good and seeking to please God. Every act we do for God in love means a new piece of treasure will be awaiting us in heaven. Thus Augustine wrote:

> Let the manner of your life be adorned by chastity, sobriety, and moderation... As to worldly riches, if you do not possess them, do not seek them by doing evil on earth, and if you possess them, let them by good works be laid up in heaven. The manly and Christian spirit should neither be elated by the acquisition of this world's treasures nor crushed by their loss. Rather, let us think of what the Lord says: "Where your treasure is, there will your heart be also" (*Letters* 189:7).

St Paul tells us that our works will be tested "by fire," and if what we have built survives the test, we will receive a reward (1 *Co* 3:10-15).

It is important to keep our focus on heaven even when we experience earthly hardship, for "the sufferings of this present time are not worth comparing with the glory that is to be revealed to us" (*Rm* 8:18), and "this slight momentary affliction is preparing for us an eternal weight of glory beyond all comparison" (2 *Co* 4:17).

The following early Christian writers and documents are quoted in this booklet.

2 *Clement* (late first century):

One of the earliest Christian writings outside the New Testament, this anonymous document was often attributed to Pope St Clement I. However, modern scholars think it was written by someone else.

Arnobius of Sicca (d. c. AD 330):

A convert from paganism who became an early Christian apologist. He lived in Sicca (modern El Kef, Tunisia).

St Augustine (AD 354-430):

A doctor of the Church and the most important Latin-speaking theologian in the age of the Fathers. He had a pagan father and a Christian mother and converted to the Faith as an adult. He became the bishop of Hippo Regius in Numidia (modern Annaba, Algeria).

Pope St Clement I (late first century):

An early pope and the author of a valuable *Letter to the Corinthians* which is one of the first surviving pieces of Christian literature outside the New Testament. Some sources say he is the same Clement that Paul mentions in Philippians 4:3.

Clement of Alexandria (c. AD 150-c. AD 214):

A layman who became a theologian and for a time headed the famous catechetical school in Alexandria, Egypt.

St Cyprian of Carthage (c. AD 205-258):
Bishop of Carthage (modern Tunis, Tunisia). He was an influential figure in North Africa and wrote many letters and treatises. Eventually, he was martyred.

St Cyril of Jerusalem (c. AD 315-386):
A doctor of the Church and a bishop of Jerusalem. He is famous for a set of catechetical lectures he gave to new converts to the Faith.

Didache (mid-first century):
The *Didache* (did-ah-KAY) is an early Church manual describing basic Christian beliefs and practices. It is one of the earliest pieces of Christian literature and appears to have been written during the apostolic age.

Hermas (late first century):
A former slave and Christian who lived in Rome and who received a series of private revelations. He recorded these in a book known as *The Shepherd*, after the guardian angel who appeared to him in the guise of a shepherd. It is one of the earliest works of Christian literature outside the New Testament.

St Gregory of Nazianz (c. AD 330-c. AD 389):
A doctor of the Church and patriarch of Constantinople. He is an important theologian and one of the three "Cappadocian Fathers," together with St Basil of Caesarea and St Gregory of Nyssa. Cappadocia is in modern Turkey.

St Ignatius of Antioch (d. c. AD 110):
A bishop of Antioch (modern Antakya, Turkey). While on his way to be martyred in Rome, he wrote a series of seven letters which provide valuable information about the Church at the dawn of the second century. His letters include the first surviving use of the term "Catholic" for the Church.

St Jerome (c. AD 347-c. AD 419):
A doctor of the Church. Originally from Dalmatia (modern Croatia), Jerome travelled widely and eventually settled in Bethlehem, where he devoted himself to scholarly pursuits. He became the foremost biblical scholar of his day, and he is most famous for translating the Vulgate, the main Latin version of the Bible.

St John Chrysostom (c. AD 359-AD 407):
A doctor of the Church and patriarch of Constantinople. He received the Greek nickname *chrusostomos* ("golden-mouthed") for his eloquence as a preacher.

Lactantius (c. AD 250-c. AD 317):
A North African student of Arnobius of Sicca, Lactantius was a tutor of Latin rhetoric. After converting to Christianity, he wrote a series of works, the most famous of which is known as the *Divine Institutes* – a systematic exposition of Christian thought.

Letter of Barnabas (late first century):
An anonymous letter that is one of the first surviving pieces of Christian literature outside the New Testament.

Historically it was often attributed to St Barnabas the apostle and companion of Paul, but modern scholars doubt this.

Oration on Simeon and Anna (date uncertain):
A Christian treatise often attributed to St Methodius of Olympia (c. AD 250-c. AD 311), though this is disputed.

Origen (c. AD 184-c. AD 254):
An early Christian writer from Alexandria, Egypt. Although some of his views were problematic, he was one of the greatest Scripture scholars of the early Church.

St Patrick (c. AD 387-c. AD 493):
Early bishop and evangelist. He was born in Great Britain but was taken captive at an early age and made a slave in Ireland. After escaping, he was led by a vision to return and proclaim the message of Christ. He thus became "the apostle of the Irish."

Tertullian of Carthage (c. AD 157-c. AD 245):
A Christian lawyer from Carthage (modern Tunis, Tunisia) who became an influential Christian writer. Although he ended up joining a schismatic sect, his writings are still valuable for what they reveal about the early Church.

Theodoret of Cyr (c. AD 393-c. AD 466):
A bishop of Cyr (near modern Kilis, Turkey). He was an active participant in the theological controversies of his day, including Nestorianism and Monophysitism, both

of which misunderstood the relationship of Christ's divine and human natures.

Translation Sources

The early Fathers wrote in a variety of languages, including Greek, Latin, and Aramaic. The translations of their writings quoted in this booklet are, for the most part, taken from a major set of volumes published more than a hundred years ago:

• The first ten volumes of this series was called *The Ante-Nicene Fathers: The Writings of the Fathers Down to AD 325*. It was edited by Rev. Alexander Roberts and James Donaldson.

• Fourteen more volumes were published under the title *A Select Library of the Nicene and Post-Nicene Fathers of the Christian Church*. These contained writings from St Augustine and St John Chrysostom, and they were edited by Philip Schaff.

• A final fourteen volumes were published under the title *A Select Library of the Nicene and Post-Nicene Fathers of the Christian Church, Series II*. These contained writings for a selection of Fathers and other ancient sources and were edited by Philip Schaff and Henry Wace.

The three sets were published between 1867 and 1900 by T. & T. Clark in Edinburgh. An American edition was published in Buffalo, New York by the Christian Literature Company. Because of when this set – commonly known as "the thirty-eight volume set" – was produced, it is in the public domain and is freely available on the Internet.

In addition to quotations from this set, a small number have been taken from other sources. These include:

◦ Richard J. Goodrich and David J. D. Miller, *St Jerome: Commentary on Ecclesiastes* (New York, The Newman Press, 2012), quoted in "When We Have Fallen."

◦ D. G. Hunter and D. H. Williams, *Hilary of Poitiers: Commentary on Matthew* (Washington, DC, The Catholic University of America Press, 2012), quoted in "Fasting."

◦ Denis J. Kavanagh, *Saint Augustine: Commentary on the Lord's Sermon on the Mount with Seventeen Related Sermons* (Washington, DC, The Catholic University of America Press, 1951), quoted in "Dealing with Anxiety."

◦ H.P.V. Nunn, *Christian Inscriptions* (London, SPCK, 1920). This work provides a helpful numbering system for some of the early Christian inscriptions found by archaeologists. It is quoted in "Helping Our Departed Loved Ones" and "Seeking Help from the Saints."

◦ Rev. Thomas Olden, *The Confession of St Patrick* (Dublin, James McGlashan, 1853), quoted in "The Religious Life."

Those translations old enough to be in the public domain contain many archaisms. Consequently, as an aide to understanding, we have updated the texts quoted from them to better conform to contemporary English usage.